Mel Bay Presents

CHANSONS
of the 16th Century
for Classical Guitar

Franco-Flemish and Parisian Chansons
Printed by Pierre Attaingnant

**Commentary, translations, and arrangements
for solo guitar or lute by Richard Metzger**

Page 79 left blank intentionally

1 2 3 4 5 6 7 8 9 0

Visit us on the Web at www.melbay.com — E-mail us at email@melbay.com

CONTENTS

ii

Commentary

The Chanson in Attaingnant Prints

Pierre Attaingnant: The Revolution in Printing and the French Chanson

Pierre Attaingnant (*c*1494 *c* late 1551 or 1552) was one of the preeminent music printers in Europe and certainly the preeminent music printer in France in the first half of the sixteenth century. He invented a technique in which the staves and notes were combined and printed in a single impression. The new process quickly supplanted double and triple-impression printing from engraved wood blocks. Single-impression printing, with its considerable reductions of cost and production time, made possible the first mass-production in music printing and afforded Attaingnant an overwhelming advantage in business over his competitors. Attaingnant developed an international network of distribution for his books. Hence the music he printed was widely disseminated in Europe. The earliest known print is the Noyon breviary of 1525.

Attaingnant's extensive catalog included liturgical books, masses, motets, chansons, danseries, lute tablatures, and keyboard scores. Throughout his thirty-year career, he concentrated on the publication of new compositions by French composers. Attaingnant was probably not a composer. He was apparently a mature musician, however, and his abilities enabled him to edit most of the music he printed. Overall, the editions were very accurate. Although Attaingnant occasionally pilfered from other printers, the body of his work was more often the target of piracy.

The collections of chansons stand among the most interesting and important editions. Attaingnant's collections record all the chanson styles of the day. Important Franco-Flemish chanson composers such as Antoine de Févin, Adrian Willaert, and Nicolas Gombert were represented, as well as the principal exponents of the Parisian chanson, Claudin de Sermisy and Clément Janequin.

Style in Attaingnant Chanson Prints: Franco-Flemish and Parisian Chansons

From a stylistic point of view, Attaingnant's first chanson collection, *Quarante et deux chansons musicales a troys parties nouvellement et correctement imprimés à Paris* (1529), contains the most mixed repertory. The compilation juxtaposed conservative polyphonic Franco-Flemish chansons with settings in transitional styles and settings akin in their treble-dominated chordal textures to the new Parisian chanson. In later collections, the Parisian chanson supplanted compositions in the older style, yet through the prints of the early 1530s, compositions extensively influenced by the Franco-Flemish chanson were included in abundant numbers. Many of the imitative chansons in anthologies of the 1530s were published without ascription to composer and were, in fact, composed by northern composers who followed the older, learned practices. Many of Attaingnant's early collections also embrace extremely interesting and attractive "hybrid" or transitional chansons such as "Vive la marguerite" and "C'est grand erreur de cuider presumer," both included in the 1529 print.

Several of the compositions in the early prints were new settings of music dating from the fifteenth century. Agricola's chanson-motet "Belle sur toutes ma doulce amye-Tota pulcra es," included in *Quarante et deux chansons musicales,* is an example. Another example of a new setting of music with origin in the previous century is Jean

Duboys' "Ma bouche rit," included in Attaingnant's 1535 print *Second livre contenant xxxi chansons musicales*. Duboys' chanson is contained in the present volume and can be compared to Johannes Ockeghem's late fifteenth-century virelai "Ma bouche rit" given as Additional Music. The texts can also be compared and are found among the translations of the poetry. Only a fragment of the first line of text is shared and the style and musical content of the settings differ significantly. Nonetheless, many of the same themes run throw each text. The text of Duboys' setting is more compact and more explicit.

The older style of composition drew its inspiration and models from the Franco-Flemish chansons of the generation of Josquin Desprez and Pierre de la Rue. Josquin's chansons, as well as those of contemporaries such as Antoine de Févin, were widely disseminated in manuscript and in the three-volume set of chansons Ottavino Petrucci printed in Italy in the years from 1501, *Odhecaton, Canti B,* and *Canti C.*

The Franco-Flemish chanson of the early sixteenth century bore several strong characteristics. Emphasis shifted among Josquin and his contemporaries from the predetermined design elements of the *formes fixes,* the *rondeau*, *ballade*, and *virelai,* to the development within the music of a single motif. The music was constructed in a series of interlocked phrases, each most often developed imitatively. Imitative exposition at the beginning of the phrase gave way to passages of polyphonic dialogue or thickly scored chords before arriving at the cadence. Cadences were often elided or constructed so that the next phrase began without pause. Hence, each cadence marked not only the end of a section but also the start of the next phrase.

Increased sensitivity was shown in the musical treatment of the text. Textures were manipulated to alter mood or express textual meaning. Unity within the musical structure was often attained by repetition, often of the first exposition or by melodic material developed in a new exposition but in a way that would not prevent recognition of the original melody.

The Franco-Flemish chanson bore similarity to the motet, differing primarily in shorter length, more tuneful melody, clearer phrase definition, lighter nature, and shorter, more definite rhythm. Examples abound in the current anthology. Gombert's "Gris et tanne" and "Pauvre coeur, tant il m'ennuie" exemplify the similarity to the motet.

Josquin and his contemporaries occasionally appropriated popular melodies sung in the streets, rather than plainsong, for use as canti firmi. Moreover, Josquin sometimes used the popular melody in canon rather than as the cantus firmus. Canonic treatment is found in "Faulte d'argent," included as Additional Music. Asterisks mark the entrances of the subject of the first exposition. The first statement of the subject, which begins in the bass of the first measure, is incomplete, breaking off on the third beat of the second measure to furnish support. The second entrance, which begins in the alto (appearing here as the higher voice) in the first measure and ends on the third beat of fifth measure, gives the complete subject. The third entrance, which begins in the soprano on the last beat of measure 5 and ends in measure 10, also states the complete subject.

Josquin and his contemporaries were also the first to draw upon a body of popular poems that circulated in France in the early sixteenth century. Later poetic song texts, especially those of Clément Marot, often mixed courtly elements with immediate, less lofty sentiments. Other texts embraced outright ribald elements and crude language. The text of "Faulte d'argent" exemplifies a low humor:

Faulte d'argent, c'est douleur non pareil,	The lack of money is sorrow without equal,
Se je le dis, las, je scay bien pourqoui,	I say it because I know well why!
Sans de quibus,	Until one lacks the means,
Il se faut tenir quoi,	One cannot truly appreciate,
Femme qui dort, pour argent se reveille.	[That] a woman who is asleep will awake for money!

Transitional pieces, such as the aforementioned "C'est grand erreur de cuider presumer," display the traits of the Franco-Flemish chanson but they differ in several respects. The imitative expositions are built on a single short motif rather than a protracted melody and are tightly regulated by the vertical considerations of harmony. Imitative expositions are abandoned in some phrases in favor of chordal textures, and non-imitative materials are repeated, sometimes immediately after the initial statement.

The motif of "C'est grand erreur," the first four notes of the soprano voice, is described as three unchanging pitches and the upward leap of the interval of a fourth. The motif is imitated quickly several times in each voice in the first four measures, inverted, and used as the basis of the second imitative exposition that begins in the sixth measure. The impression, however, is not one of imitative exposition constructed of extended melody but of two successive chord progressions with simple melodic fragments passed among the voices. The effect of progression is enhanced by the sequences of V-I root motion, a function of the motif, in the bass.

The Parisian chanson, which emerged in the late 1520s and predominated through the 1530s and 1540s, stands in sharp contrast to the Franco-Flemish chanson. The composers of the Parisian chanson largely abandoned the complex imitative polyphony and interlocking-phrase structure of the Franco-Flemish chanson. As a general practice, the leading composers, Claudin de Sermisy and Clément Janequin, favored instead textures in which a finely turned and sometimes lyrical melody was supported by simple chords. The treble-dominated texture was enlivened by occasional imitative snatches that did not compromise the homophonic texture, by intermittent melismatic fragments at pause points in the line, or by brief activity in a voice other than the soprano. The musical scaffold was often a duet between the soprano and tenor voices. The bass voice sometimes merely offered support, although it sometimes participated in ornamentation. Frequently the alto voice was a perfunctory part with a purely harmonic function.

The phrase structure of the music adhered to the phrase structure of the poetic text. The poems were often strophic. Uniform text phrase length and repeated poetic rhythms in the text were mirrored in the music, often creating musical rhythms that marked each phrase. A frequently cited but nonetheless still charming example of the Parisian chanson is Sermisy's "Tant que vivray," presented as Additional Music. The rhythm that begins each line, half note-quarter note-quarter note, mirrors the text rhythm and is also a common component of many chansons regardless of the style in which they were composed. Attaingnant printed the lute setting of "Tant que vivray" in *Trés familiere introduction pour entendre & apprendre par soi mêmes a jour toutes chansons reduictes en la tabulature du Lutz...*(Paris, 1529).

Sermisy was a master of the delicate and sophisticated love song. Janequin, on the other hand, often imbued his music with irreverent, even occasionally rowdy, humor. An example of Janequin's humor is seen in the text to "Un jour Colin la Colette" a chanson printed in *Tresiésme livre contenant xxi chansons musicales à quatres parties en ung volume et en deux. Imprimées par Pierre Attaingnant et Hubert Jullet...1543:*

Un jour Colin la Colette accula,
En lui disant, "or mettez le cul là,"
Puis de si prés,
Se prit à l'accoler,
Qu'en l'accolant,
Qu'en bricolant,
La goutte fit couler,
Et pour culer,
Jamais ne recula.

One day Colin the Prude drove to a halt,
Saying to her, "now put your backside there,"
Ever so close,
He put his arms around her neck,
That embracing her,
Alarming her,
The taste was made to flow,
And as for pulling away,
She never did draw back.

Janequin also composed chansons with narrative texts. Narrative text is exemplified in "Martin menait son proceau" a chanson printed in *Tiers livre contenant xxi chansons musicales à quatres parties composez par Jennequin & Passereau [imprimée] par Pierre Attaingnant...Mense Mayo M.D. xxxvi* [1536]:

Martin menait son porceau au marché,
Avec Alix qui en la plaine grande,
Pria Martin de faire le píche de l'un sur l'autre,

Et Martin lui demande,
"Et qui tiendra notre porceau friande,

"Qui," dit Alix, "Bon reméde il ya,"
Lors le porceau à sa jambe lia,
Et Martin juche qui lourdement engaine,
Le porc eut peur et Alix s'écria,
"Serre, Martin, notre porceau m'entraine."

Martin drove his pig to market,
With Alex who in the big field,
Entreated Martin to snatch a peach by standing piggy-back,
And Martin asked him.
"And who will hold our dainty pig?"

"Who?" says Alex, "here is a good solution."
Then he tied the pig to his leg,
And Martin climbed clumsily upon his shoulders.
The pig became frightened and Alex cried out,
"Hold tight, Martin, our pig is dragging me away!"

Jannequin is best known, however, for long, descriptive chansons in which the themes permitted the musical depiction of birdsong, street cries, battle sounds, and the like.

Translations of the Chanson Texts and their Print Sources

Poetry from Attaingnant Prints

Although the present volume contains only instrumental settings, understanding the poetic text offers information invaluable to correct musical realization. The texts also offer insight into life in another time, though somehow universal to our own.

Three-voice chansons

Quarante et deux chansons musicales à troys parties nouvellement et correctement imprimées à Paris le xxii jour d'arpil mil cinq centz vingt et neuf par Pierre Attaingnant [1529].

1. Ce n'est pas, certes

Ce n'est pas, certes, gloire chevaleureuse,
De decepvoir jeune pucelle honteuse,
Et si je t'ay aymé sans refuser,
Ma simplesse bien me doit excuser,
Tu m'as vaincue,
Mais quoi, j'estoye femme,
Et surprise de l'amoureuse flamme

There is no chivalry to be sure,
In deceiving a young, embarrassed virgin,
And if I have loved you without refusing
My naivete then must be my excuse.
You have made me your conquest,
But then, I am only a woman,
And one ambushed by love's flame.

2. C'est grand erreur de cuider présumer

C'est grand erreur de cuider présumer,
Qu'on peult hanter prés de la creature,
En devisant des oeuvres de nature,
Sans que le feu se voulsist allumer.

It is a great mistake to assume,
That one who can press near the creature,
And talk of the ways of nature,
Without igniting its spark.

3. Le cueur is mien

Le cueur is mien qui oncques ne fut pris,
Fors en ung lieu ou il fait sa demeure,
Et y sera jusques a ce qu'il meure,
Car de long temps l'a ainsi entrepris.

My heart is mine and was never taken captive,
Except in one small place deep inside,
And will live there until it dies,
For a long time I have felt it.

Sur tous amans il emporte le pris,
Car nuyt et jour il ne se passe une heure,
Qu'a bien aymer son esprit ne labeure:
Or devinez s'Amours l'en ont promis.

Above all lovers it holds the prize,
Because night and day an hour does not pass,
That its spirit does not labor in love.
Guess what love has promised!

Par terre et mer, sans nul mettre a despris,
Vive celuy qui tant a l'amour seuere,
Qui d'Atropos mieulx vouldroit la morsure
Qu'en faulce amour il eust esté repris.

By land and sea, without granting any hope,
Lives he who as long as love is assured him,
Would like better the bite of Death,
Than find himself caught in false love's trap,

Puis donc qu'en toy tant de biens sont compris,
En esperant que Amours me sequeure
De t'oublier, pour quelques temps qui queure,
De te changer je n'ay point aprins.

Because in you there is so much good,
And I hope that love will save me,
From forgetting you as time goes by,
And quitting you I have not yet learned.

4. D'amour je suis déshéritée

D'amour je suis déshéritée,
Complaindre ne me scay à qui,
Helas, j'ai perdu mon amy,
Seulette suis, il m'a laissée.

Ne suis je pas bien fortunée?
Quant à l'aymer, je consenty;
Helas, je luy fist bon party,
Dont je suis mal recompensée.

Je luys avovye m'amour donnée,
Mais par le mauvistié de luy,
Helas, il s'en est desaisy,
Trop rudement in m'a traictée.

A l'appetit d'une affettée
Qui sans cesser mesdit d'aultruy,
Helas, je suis mise en oubly,
Parqouy ju suis à mort livrée.

From love I am estranged,
And don't know to whom I should complain,
Alas, I lost my love,
I am alone; he left me.

Am I not lucky?
When to love, I consented,
Alas, I gave the best part,
For which I am ill repaid.

I gave him my love,
But by his mal-intent,
Alas, he forfeits it,
Too rudely has he treated me.

The desires of one smitten,
Who without relief slandered me,
So I am forgotten,
And am delivered unto death.

5. Je brusle et ars

Je brusle et ars est mon cueur espris,
Comme le souffre qui le feu est espris;
Entends pour vray, quant je dors ou je veille,
J'ay le tien nom toujours en mon oreille.

I burn – aflame is my heart,
Like sulfur the fire burns,
Understand truly, when I sleep or wake,
I have your name ringing in my ears.

Antoine de Févin

6. On a mal dit de mon amy

On a mal dit de mon amy,
Dont j'ai le coeur triste et marri,
Mais qu'en ont ils affaire,
Ou s'il est beau ou s'il est laid,
Puis qu'il est bien à mon plaisir.

They speak poorly of my friend,
Hence I have a sad and aggrieved heart,
But that is their affair,
Whether he is handsome or he is ugly,
Since he suits my pleasure.

7. Le trop long temps

Le trop long temps qu'ay esté sans te veoir
A le mien cueur blessé de telle sorte,
Qu'esse voulu mille fois estre morte
Si bon espoir n'y eust voulu pourveoir.

The long time since I have not seen you,
Has wounded my heart,
It would be better to be dead a thousand times,
If hope did not ease my longing.

8. Trop se fier

Trop se fier aux promesses d'aultruy
N'est seureté ou il y a durée;
Trop esperer chose non asseurée
M'ont amené ou Langeur m'entretient:
Trop est roti qui à la grille tient.

Too trusting in the promises of others,
There is no guarantee over time,
Too hopeful of something not assured,
I have arrived at a state of listlessness;
He is roasted who hangs over the fire.

9. Vive la marguerite

Vive la marguerite, c'est une noble fleur
Pourtant s'elle est petit, elle est de grant valeur,
Qui voudra s'en despite, je luy portray honneur:
Vive la marguerite, c'est une noble fleur.

Long live the daisy; she is a noble flower
For so much as she is little, she still has great value
Let who will be offended: I will honor her,
Long live the daisy; she is a noble flower.

Four-voice chansons

Trente et quatre chansons musicales à quatres parties imprimée à Paris le xxiii jour de janvier mil.v.c.xxviii par Pierre Attaingnant [1528].

10. Amour et mort me font outrage

(text: Clément Marot)

Amour et mort me font outrage,	Love and death outrage me
Amour me retient en servage,	Love holds me in bondage,
Et mort, accroître ce deuil,	And death, increasing this sorrow,
A pris celui loin de mon oeil,	Has taken him far from my sight,
Qui de prés navre mon courage.	Who when close distressed my heart.

Trente et huyt chansons musicales à quatres parties nouvellement imprimée par Pierre AttaingnantÖkal.ianua 1529.

11. Gris et tanne me faut porter

Nicolas Gombert

Gris et tanne me faut porter,	Gray and tan must sustain me,
Car tanne suis en espérance,	For tan gives me hope,
Le jaune me convient laisser,	Yellow abandons me,
Car c'est le couleur de jouissance,	Because it is the color of joyfulness,
Le noir si est significance,	Black, if it has significance,
De vivre en deuil ma maîtresse,	It is of my mistress living in mourning,
Puis qu'il convient que je vous laisse.	Since the time comes that I must leave.

Six gaillardes et six pavanes avec treze chansons musicales à quatres parties imprimées à Paris par Pierre Attaingnant...1529.

12. À l'aventure l'enterpris

Adrian Willaert

À l'aventure l'enterpris,	To the experience of the endeavor,
Cuidant gagner enfin de prix,	To gain at last the prize
Pour ma maîtresse bien aimer,	Of loving well my mistress,
Si l'ai seri sur terre et mer,	I have served her on land an sea,
Mais j'ai mon temps mis,	I have put all my time,
Tout compris à l'aventure,	Completely devoted to the experience,
J'ai pour chassé ce qu'autre a pris,	I have pursued that which another already holds,
Mon réconfort du tout m'est pris,	My reconciliation is taken,
Dont mon coeur est confit d'aimer,	From whom my heart is reserved to love,
À l'aventure,	For the experience.
Je ne serais jamais repris,	I will never be enamored of another,
Tant que je vive en ce pour pris,	As long as I live dedicated to this purpose,
Qu'en rien ne la veux déprimer,	Nothing about her discourages yearning,
Mais en mon coeur fort imprimer,	But pressed into my heart,
Qu'à tort bani suis et dépris,	Forbidden injury follows and is exiled,
Par qoui ravis sont mes esprits,	And my spirits are ravished,
À l'aventure.	By the experience.

13. En l'ombre d'un buissonet

Mathieu Lasson

En l'ombre d'un buissonet,
Tout au long d'une riviére
J'ai trouvé le fils Marquet,
Qui priait sa dame chére,
Disant en cette maniére,
"Je vous jure, fin couer doux,
Et je vous aime, fin coeur doux,"
A donc répond la bergére,
"Robin, comment l'entendez vous?"

In the shade of a hedge,
That runs along a stream,
I found the son Marquet,
Begging to his dear woman,
Saying in this way,
"I swear to you, fine sweet heart,
I love you, fine sweet heart,"
To which the shepherdess replies,
"Robin, how do you know that?"

Trente et six chansons musicales à quatres parties imprimée à Paris par Pierre Attaingnant...1530.

14. Jamais je n'aimerai grand homme

Jamais je n'aimerai grand homme,
J'aimerai un petit homme
Le petit serre de prés,
Tu dissais que j'en mourais,
Menteuse, f,cheuse,
Que tu es.

I will never love an important man,
I will love a humble man,
The humble one does not stray.
You say that I will perish by him,
Liar, troublemaker,
That you are.

15. Tous compagnons qui beuvez volontiers

Tous compagnons qui beuvez volontiers,
À celui qui a fait la chanson,
Vous faites mal,
Si vous ne presentez,
Du bon vin et d'un gras chapon.

All companions who drink willingly,
To he who made the song:
You offend,
If you do not present
Some good wine and a fat capon.

Livre premier contenant xxix. chansons musicales à quatres parties imprimée par Pierre Attaingnant...Mense Januario M.D. xxxv [1535].

16. Aprés avoir las tout mon temps passé

Pierre Certon

Aprés avoir las tout mon temps passé,
En deuil et peine,
En travail et tristesse,
Servant le mieux que je peux ma maîtresse,
Est-ce raison que j'en sois de chasse.

All my time is spent,
In mourning and grief,
In travail and sadness,
Serving as best I can my mistress,
Why did I want her so?

17. Nature a fait, ainsi Dieu

Roquelay

Nature a fait,
Ainsi Dieu l'a permis,
Ton trés gent corps et amoureuse face,
À celle fin que dure mort efface,
Mon trist coeur a ton vouloir soumis.

Nature made it,
Thus God permitted it,
Your very noble body and loving face,
To that end which harsh death effaces them,
My sad heart to your desire submits.

Premier livre contenant xxxi chansons musicales esleves de plusiers livres par ci devant imprimez: et naugeres reprimées en ung volume par Pierre Attaingnant...Mense Februario M.D. xxxv [1535].

18. Joie et douleur, mon ami   Guillaume Ysoré

Joie et douleur, mon ami,	Joy and sadness, my love,
Sur mon ,me,	On my soul,
C'est de te voir,	Is to see you,
Car il n'est nulle le dame,	Because no other woman,
Qui aime plus son ami prés de soi,	Loves her lover more than I,
Et puis Dieu sait quelle douleur reçois,	And since God knows what sadness is received,
Quand pour t'aimer tant à tort,	Loving you to a fault,
On me bl,me, à tort,	One blames me, I am wrong,
Quand pour t'aime.	For loving you so.

Second livre contenant xxxi chansons musicales esleves de plusiers livres par ci devant imprimez: et naugeres reprimées en ung volume par Pierre Attaingnant...Mense Februario M.D. xxxv [1535].

19. Ma bouche rit   Jean Duboys

Ma bouche rit et mon coeur pleure,	My mouth laughs and my heart cries,
Quand j'ai perçois ma dame à l'heure,	At the time when I perceive that my love,
Qu'entre les gens prend ces soulas,	Among others takes solace,
Mais à part je lui dis,	But in private I tell her,
HÈlas, belle ne souffrez que je meure."	"Alas, your beauty will tolerate only that I die."

Tiers livre contenant xxi chansons musicales à quatres parties composez par Jennequin & Passereau [imprimée] par Pierre Attaingnant...Mense Mayo M.D. xxxvi [1536].

20. Il n'est plaisir ni passetemps   Clément Janequin

Il n'est plaisir ni passetemps au monde,	There is neither pleasure nor pastime in the world,
Que de bergerie,	Of the sheepfold,
Quand on est par bois ou par champs,	When one is in the woods or in the fields,
Chantant, dansant, riant, à son amie,	Singing, dancing, laughing with her love,
La droguette, godinet, jolie, jolie,	The woolen blanket, country lass, pretty, pretty,
Au monde n'a rien si plaisant,	In the world there is nothing so pleasant
Il n'est plaisir ni passetemps.	There is neither pleasure nor pastime

21. Notre dince, mon compère   Clément Janequin

Notre dince, mon compère,	Since our wedding, my fellow,
Que votre chose est petit,	Your thing is so small!
Si vous n'en voulez rien faire,	If you don't want to do anything about it,
Je perdrai mon appetit,	I will lose my desire.
Le jour qu'on nous maria,	The day we married,
Vous et moi tous deux ensemble,	You and I became one,
Je dis Jesus Maria de la peur que j'eus tremble,	I said Jesus, Mary from the fear in which I trembled,
Mais par mon ,me il me semble,	But by my soul it seems to me,
Qu'il n'est pas vrai ce qu'on dit,	That it is not true what they say,
Qu'on trouve les femmes mortes,	That one finds his wife dead,
Le premier jour dans leur lit,	The first day in their bed.

Notre dince, mon compère,
Que votre chose est petit,
Si vous n'en voulez rien faire,
Je perdrai mon appetit.

Since our wedding, my fellow,
Your thing is so small!
If you don't want to do anything about it,
I will lose my desire.

Tresième livre xix. chansons nouvelles à quatre parties en ung volume et en deux.
Imprimée par Pierre Attaingnant et Hubert Jullet ...1543.

22. Un jour un gallant engrossa

Pierre Certon

Un jour un gallant engrossa,
D'un coup une jeune pucelle,
Dont le ventre qui se haussa,
Découvrit la charge nouvelle,
Et puis et puis quand on lui dit la belle,
"Comment avez vous fait cela?"
"Jamais n'eusse cru," se dit elle,
"Que vaut ce petit membre là."

On day a gallant made pregnant
In a single conquest a young virgin,
Whose belly began to swell.
No longer permitting disguise of the new burden.
By and by people began to question little beauty,
"How did that happen?"
"It could never have grown," she said,
"From that little limb!"

Trente chansons musicales à quatres parties nouvellement et tres correctement imprimée
à Paris par Pierre Attaingnant...n.d.

23. Pauvre coeur, tant il m'ennuie

Pauvre coeur, tant il m'ennuie,
Je ne sais que devenir,
Pour la belle qui tant j'aimoye,
Qui m'a planté pour reverdir,
À l'aventure,
Hé mon ami, le souvenir de vous me tue,

Poor heart, as long as it engulfs me,
I don't know what to do,
For the beauty who I love,
Who abandoned me in the country to revive
His sense of adventure.
Alas, my love, the memory of you kills me.

C'est à Paris,
La jolie ville,
Qu'on dit que nos amours sont,
Mais nous ne les perdrons mie,
Si ce n'est par trahison,
À l'aventure,
HÈ mon ami, le souvenir de vous me tue.

It is in Paris,
The beautiful city
Where they say love is,
But we will not lose love, my love,
If you do not betray me,
For the sake of adventure,
Alas, my love, the memory of you kills me.

Trente et quatre chansons musicales à quatres parties imprimée à Paris par Pierre
Attaingnant...n.d.

24. Apporte à boire

Apporte à boire du salé,
Et du vin blanc de gourde de pié,
Qui engendre aux yeux la roupié,
Quand on en a bien avalé,
Au plus soudain du feu, du pain.
Tire nous pinte et le fait court,
Verse tout plein le verre en main,
Chantons tous, donnez nous du gourd.

Bring to the table some salt pork,
And some white wine from the charitable bottle,
That brings contentment to the eyes,
When one has well drunk down,
At once the warmth of the fire, some bread,
To hold a pint and make it empty,
Fill the glass in hand,
We all sing, give us the bottle!

25. Reveillez vous, jeunes dames qui dormez

Reveillez vous, jeunes dames qui dormez,
Et pour amoureux priez,
Que Dieu leur doit soulas et joie,
Il fait bon dormir sur un lit,
Entre les bras de son ami,
Quand on y prend soulas et joie.
Rossignolet du bois joli,
Otez ami de souci,
Et l'amenez sans qu'on la voie,
Tres doux penser Dieu te pour voie.

Wake up young sleeping girls!
And for love pray,
That God gives solace and joy,
It bodes well to sleep on a bed.
In the arms of your lover,
There one finds solace and joy.
The little nightingale of the pretty woods,
Takes away the cares of your lover,
And brings contentment,
Think sweetly of God for good fortune.

Poetry from Other Sources

Ottavino Petrucci, *Odhecaton* (1501).

26. Johannes Ockegham, "Ma bouche rit"

Ma bouche rit et ma pensée pleure,
Mon oeil s'esjoie et mon cueur maudit l'eure.
Qu'il eust le bien qui sa santé déchasse,
Et le plaisir que la mort me pour chasse,
Sans réconfort qui m'aide ne sequeure.

My mouth laughs and my heart cries,
My eye rejoices and my heart curses the hour,
Since it is pleasure that destroys my health,
And through pleasure that death pursues me,
Without consolation to aid or insulate me.

Ha, cueuer pervers, faulsaire et mensongier,
Dictes tes comment avez osé songier,
Que de faulcer ce que m'avez promis?

Ah, perverse, false, and lying heart,
Tell how you dared to dream,
You could deny me what you have promised?

Puis qu'en ce point vous vous volez vengier,
Pensez bientost de ma vie abregier,
Vivre ne puis au point où m'avez mis.

Since on this point you wish revenge,
Think soon of cutting short my life,
So I live no longer in the life you have placed me,

Vestre pitié veult doucques que je meure,
Mais rigeur veult que vivant je demeure,
Ainsi meurs vif, et en vivant trespasse,
Mais pour ceter le mal qui ne se passe,
Et pur couvrir le deul ou je labeure.

Your pity desires that I die,
But decorum demands that living I remain,
Thus dying live and in living transgress,
Only to hide the unceasing pain,
And disguise the sorrow that burdens me.

Ma bouche rit et ma pensée pleure,
Mon oeil s'esjoie et mon cueur maudit l'eure.
Qu'il eust le bien qui sa santé déchasse,
Et le plaisir que la mort me pour chasse,
Sans réconfort qui m'aide ne sequeure.

My mouth laughs and my thoughts cry,
My eye rejoices and my heart curses the hour,
That it is pleasure that destroys my health,
And through pleasure that death pursues me,
Without consolation to aid or insulate me.

27. Josquin Desprez, "Faulte d'argent" (For text see p.v above)

28. Claudin de Sermisy, "Tant que vivray"

The lute setting of "Tant que vivray" appears in Attaingnant's
Trés familiere introduction pour entendre & apprendre par soi mímes a jour toutes chansons reduictes en la tabulature du Lutz...(Paris, 1529).

Tant que vivray en age florissant,	As long as I live and am able,

Tant que vivray en age florissant,
Je serviray d'amour le Dieu puissant,
En faitz, en dits, en chansons et acordz.

Par plusiers jours m'a tenu languissant,
Mais aprés dueil m'a fait réjouissant,
Cay j'ay l'amour de la belle au gent corps.

Son alliance,
C'est ma fiance,
Son cueur is mien,
Le mien est sien,
Fy de tristesse,
Vive liesse,
Puis qu'on amours, a tant de bien.

As long as I live and am able,
I will serve love, God willing,
In deed, word, song and harmony.

For many days I languished,
But later mourning turned to rejoicing,
For I have the love of a gentle beauty.

Our alliance,
She's my betrothed,
Her heart is mine,
My heart is hers,
Shunning sadness,
Embracing life,
When one loves, he has so much joy.

Biographical Sketches of the Composers in the Attaingnant Prints

Franco-Flemish Composers

<u>Johannes Ockegham</u> (*c*1410-1497). Ockegham was one of the most important composers of the second half of the fifteenth century and the most important composer of the first generation of Franco-Flemish composers. Busnois was possibly his mentor. Dufay, Busnois, and Ockegham are believed to have been more than casual acquaintances. In the 1440s Ockegham entered service at the court of Duke Charles I and remained in service in France until his death. He entered the service of Charles VII around 1451 and continued in service through the reign of Louis XI. He became canon at the cathedral of Notre Dame in Paris in 1463.

Ockegham composed masses, motets, and chansons. The chansons were composed in the *formes fixes,* in use for at least a century previous. Ockegham favored the rondeau, but four of the chansons, including "Ma bouche rit," were composed in the abbreviated virelai form also favored by Busnois. His chansons feature treble-dominanted texture and often embrace imitative writing. In "Ma bouche rit," imitation is restricted to the opening of the first line.

<u>Josquin Desprez</u> (c1440-1521). Josquin was one of the most important composers of the Renaissance. A Frenchman, he spent a significant portion of his professional life in Italy. Josquin sang at the Milan Cathedral from 1459-72. He served at the papal chapel in Rome from 1486 to *c*1501, His tenure at Ferrara around 1503 was probably cut short by his choice to flee the outbreak of plague. From 1504 until 1521, Josquin served at Notre Dame at Condé.

Josquin's compositions circulated Europe, in part promoted by the publication by Petrucci of three volumes of music, and became models for succeeding generations of composers. Collections of Josquin's music, including one by Attaingnant in 1550, were printed and disseminated posthumously. Févin and Mouton, who possibly have studied with Josquin, were notable emulators of Josquin's musical style. Josquin's innovations include the use of motives closely related to the rhythms of the text, textures of pervasive imitation, and a shift in emphasis to the musical expression of the meaning of the text. Josquin compositions include masses, motets, and chansons.

Antoine de Févin (c1470-d1511 or 1512). Févin, who came from the nobility, was a priest, singer, and composer. The writings of theorist Glarean contain two references to Févin, one as "composer of Orleans," doubtless after Févin's association with the royal court there, and the other as "follower of Josquin." Févin, in fact, was a practitioner of the new style that emerged about 1490 in the music of Josquin, Pierre de la Rue, Jean Mouton, and others. The new style is described above as the Franco-Flemish chanson.

Regard for Févin is evident in the fact that Petrucci dedicated a printed volume to his masses (ten survive). His progressive musical tendencies are seen in his reliance in the masses and motets on parody rather than cantus firmus techniques. Yet his three-voice chansons, written for entertainment at the court of Louis XII, rely almost exclusively upon the presentation in the tenor of an unadorned borrowed popular melody.

Nicolas Gombert (c1495-c1560). Gombert was probably born in Flanders and served as a cleric, perhaps priest, at Courtrai, Béthune, Lens, and Metz. Gombert was a singer in the chapel of Emperor Charles V and from 1529 the maître des enfants. References from 1534 onward identify him as a canon at Notre Dame, Tournai. The theorist Hermann Finck identifies Gombert as a student of Josquin, though possibly during Josquin's late years at Condé.

Gombert's music is characterized by use of pervading imitation, each phrase developed with its own motif. Gombert rarely used chordal passages. For contrast, Gombert varied texture by varying the number of voices. In Gombert's music, each voice is regarded as equal in importance although the bass sometimes supplied harmonic support at cadences. Like Ockeghem, he preferred the rich, dark sonority of voice parts in the lower ranges.

Ten of Gombert's masses survive. All his masses but two are based on existing motets or chansons. Gombert composed motets (160 survive), regarded as the most representative works, as well as more than seventy secular chansons. The chansons are musically similar to the Netherlands motet in their pervasive imitation and scope but differ in that they are lighter in character. His chansons are often drawn upon folk-like texts and, unlike the music of Josquin, the music does not use word-painting to illuminate textual meaning. Gombert is not the same 'Nicolas Gombert' of the Parisian chanson prints of 1547 and 1572.

Adrian Willaert (c1490-1562). Like Josquin, Willaert was one of the major composers of his time. Born in Bruges or Roulaers and trained in music in Paris by Jean Mouton, Willaert's career unfolded primarily in Italy. For a time he served as singer in Ferrara and Milan. He became maestro di cappella to St. Mark's in Venice in 1527. He remained until 1560. His duties also included teaching music, and his students included some for the most important composers and theorists of the century. Notable among his students are Zarlino, Cipriano de Rore, Nicola Vincentino, and Andrea Gabrieli.

Willaert supplied an important musical bridge between Josquin and Lassus and Palestrina. His works include masses (nine), motets, hymns, psalms, motets, madrigals, and chansons. The masses exhibit strongly the influences of Josquin and Mouton.

Although he was a major figure in chanson composition, his work is not extensively represented in the collections of Attaingnant but by chanson collections printed in Italy.

Composers of Parisian Chansons

Claudin de Sermisy (c1490-1562). Sermisy composed masses, motets, and chansons but stands as one of the most important figures in the development of the Parisian chanson. Sermisy was a singer in the chapel under Louis II. He became *sous-maître* under Francis I and retained the post under Henry II. In 1533, Sermisy was appointed as canon at Sainte-Chapelle. His printed output of chansons numbers about one hundred-sixty.

Sermisy's chansons are treble-dominated and chordal in texture. They feature charming and delicate melodies. Attention is paid to the meter of the poetry and the text is most often syllabically set with occasional ornamentation at phrase ends. As noted, many of the chasons are essentially soprano-tenor duets with obligatory bass support and almost optional alto parts.

Clément Janequin (c1485-c1558). Janequin was a composer and priest who held minor clerical positions throughout his life. From 1505 to 1523, he served Lancelot de Fau, the Bishop of Luçon from 1515. From 1523 to 1529, Janequin served the Bishop of Bordeaux. He completed his studies to become a priest in the same year he entered the bishop's service. After the death of the Bishop in 1529, the church authorities vacated all prebends. Finding himself unemployed, Janequin moved to Angers to join his brother. From 1534 to 1537 Janequin served as *maître de chapelle* at Angers. Financial difficulties, which plagued Janequin's entire life, became acute in the years between 1537 and the 1550s and an unpaid loan resulted in a complete break with his family. In the 1550s Janequin became *chantre ordinaire du Roi* and later *compositeur ordinaire du Roi*. The posts provided financial security in the last years of his life.

Janequin's chansons (over 250), psalms settings, and *chasons spirituelles* (150) overshadow his two masses, both of which are closely based on his own chansons. Janequin and Claudin de Sermisy were the most important cultivators of the Parisian chanson. While Sermisy excelled at sophisticated and delicate love songs, Janequin's reputation was built on narrative and descriptive program pieces of popular appeal and irreverent wit and humor.

The program pieces, which include "Le chant des oiseaux," "L'alouette," "La bataille," "La chasse," and "Les cries de Paris," are fraught with onomatopoeic devices. Battle cries, street cries, birdsong, fanfares, and other generally non-musical sounds are captured in the music by simple melodic motives. His shorter, non-programmatic chansons often set witty and sometimes ribald poetry. He favored rustic characters and settings in many chansons, and dialogue is a frequent component. More so than his contemporaries, Janequin paid detailed attention to the musical realization of the rhythms of the words. The settings often resulted in accents that did not fall correctly within the measure and metric shifts between duple and triple.

Composers in Hybrid Styles

Guillaume Ysoré (d1563). Ysoré, like so many of his contemporaries, was a cleric. He assumed a post as singer at Sainte-Chapelle in 1522, taking his clerical vows in 1526. By 1543 he became chaplain at St. Louis.

Only eight chansons survive. All but two were written for four voices and all but one appeared in the 1530s. The chansons show a variety of styles rather than an adherence to the single stylistic model of the Parisian chanson. The three-voice chansons differ from the four-voice in that they utilize materials borrowed from Sermisy and Jacotin.

Pierre Certon (*d* Paris 1572). Certon was appointed to the post of master of the choir at Sainte-Chapelle in 1536 and held the post until his death. The honorary title of "chantre de la chapelle du Roy" was bestowed in 1567. The title page of his 1570 chanson collection gives his title as "compositeur de la musique de la chapelle du Roy." Certon composed masses (eight survive), motets, psalms, *chansons spirituelles*, and secular chansons. His early chansons show the influence of Sermisy. The later chansons, written contemporaneously to those of Costeley and Lassus, are very progressive in regard to musical texture, the rhythmic nuances of the poetry, and the meaning of the text.

Mathieu Lasson (*d*1595). Lasson served as canon of St. Georges, Nancy and as *maître de chapelle* to the Duke of Lorraine. He assumed the post of rector of the hospital at Notre Dame, Pont à Mousson, in 1543. His fame rests on relatively few works. Five motets were printed and reprinted in France, Italy, and Germany. Only four chansons survive. The best known, "En l'ombre d'un buissonet," is contained in the present anthology. Hans Gerle set the chanson for lute in *Tabulatur auff die Laute etlicher Preambel, Teutscher, Welscher ünd Fransösischer stück* (1533).

Editorial Note

The spirit and methods of an important sixteenth-century lute tradition live in the arrangements in the present volume. Throughout the century lutenists customarily arranged vocal works to play on the instrument. The arrangements for lute, called *intabulations*, added significantly to the repertory and extended the life span of many of the compositions. Lute settings of chansons, often featuring variations by their arranger-composers, are found in manuscript and in French, Italian, and Spanish prints.

The chansons found in this anthology are modern settings. They were transcribed, however, in accordance with rules furnished by mid-sixteenth-century French tutors on the subject. The primary guidance was Adrian LeRoy's *A Briefe and plain instruction to set all musicke of diverse tunes in tablature for the lute,* a tutor translated into English and reprinted in 1574 in London by James Rowbothome. Although the pieces of the anthology are intended for guitar, the tuning of the third string to F# not only promotes the integrity of the voicing, but also permits the realization of the music on the guitar or on the lute in the *vieille ton.*

As noted, clues regarding the tempi of the chansons are offered by their texts. Many of the chansons are written in 4/4 as a matter of convenience in notation but benefit musically from later conversion to 2/2. Despite considerable imitation in many of the pieces, most of the chansons should not be heavy in character. Hence I suggest as a basic median tempo, adjustable as the music requires, of the half note=72.

Bibliography

Adams, Courtney S. *The Three-Part Chanson During the Sixteenth Century: Changes in its Style and Importance.* Unpublished Ph.D. diss., University of Pennsylvania, 1974.

Agnel, Aimé. "Pierre Certon." *New Grove* IV, 80-2.

Apel, Willi and Archibald T. Davison, eds. *Historical Anthology of Music: Oriental, Medieval, and Renaissance Music.* Cambridge, Mass.: Harvard, 1972.

Berstein, Lawrence F. "Guillaume Ysoré." *New Grove* XX, 583-4.

Brown, Howard Mayer. *Instrumental Music Printed Before 1600.* Cambridge, Mass.: Harvard, 1967.

_____ "Antoine de Févin." *New Grove* VI, 515-7.

Bruger, Hans Dagobert, ed. *Pierre Attaingnant: Zwei und dreistimmige Solostücke für die Laute.* Zürich: Möseler Verlag, 1926.

Expert, Henry and Aimé Agnel, eds. *Pierre Certon: Chansons polyphoniques publiées par Pierre Attaingnant, Livre II (1540-1545).* Paris: Heugel, 1968.

Heartz, Daniel. "Pierre Attaingnant." *New Grove* I, 673-6.

Lockwood, Lewis and Jessie Ann Owens. "Adrian Willaert." *New Grove* XX, 421-8.

Nugent, George. "Nicolas Gombert." *New Grove* VII, 512-6.

Perkins, Leeman L. "Johannes Ockeghem." *New Grove* XIII, 489-96.

Reese, Gustave. *Music in the Renaissance.* New York: Norton, 1959.

_____ and Jeremy Noble. "Josquin Desprez." *New Grove* IX, 713-38.

Sadie, Stanley, ed. *New Grove Dictionary of Music and Musicians.* London: Macmillan, 1980.

Seay, Albert, ed. *Thirty Chansons for Three and Four Voices from Attaingnant's Collections.* New Haven, Conn.: Yale, 1960.

Thomas, Bernard, ed. *The Parisian Chanson: Thirty Chansons (1529) for Three Instruments or Voices,* v.10. London: London Pro Musica Edition, 1977.

Vaccaro, Jean-Michel. *La Chanson à la Renaissance.* Tours: Éditions van de Velde, 1981.

Chansons from Attaingnant Prints

1. Ce n'est pas, certes

2. C'est grand erreur de cuider presumer

4

III---

3. Le cueur est mien

③ = F#

4. D'amour je suis desheritee

8

5. Je brusle et ars

6. On a mal dit de mon ami

Antoine de Fevin

Vihuela belonging to Maestro Emilio Pujol (1886-1980)
constructed by Spanish luthier Miguel Simplicio. This
instrument is a copy of the only known extant example of a
sixteenth century vihuela discovered by Pujol in 1936 at
the Jacquert-André Museum in Paris.

7. Le trop long temps

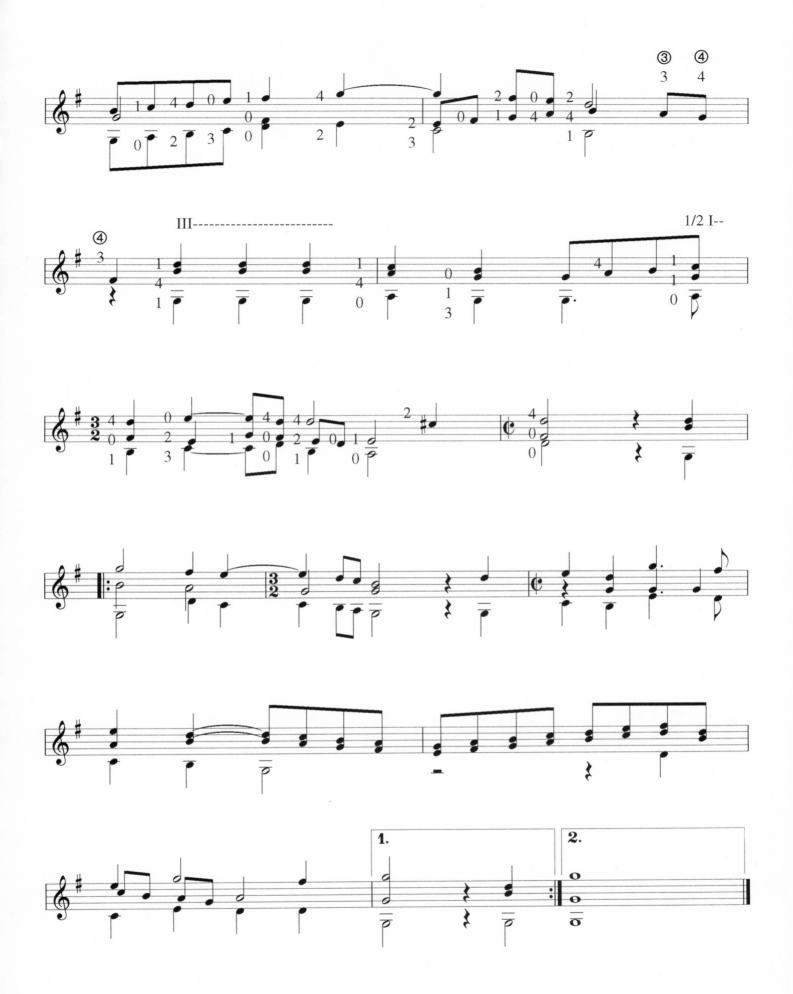

8. Trop se fier

9. Vive la Marguerite

10. Amour et mort me font outrage

11. Gris et tanne me faut porter

Nicolas Gombert

12. A l'aventure l'enterpris

Adrian Willaert

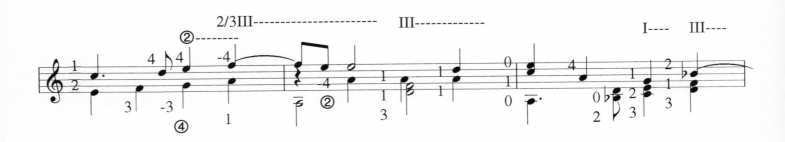

13. En l'ombre d'un buissonet

Mathieu Lasson

14. Jamais je n'aimerai grand homme

Rosette of a Baroque lute.

15. Tous compagnons qui beuvez volontiers

16. Apres avoir las tout mon temps passe

Pierre Certon

17. Nature a fait, ainsi Dieu

Roquelay

18. Joie et douleur, mon ami

Guillaume Ysore

③ = F#

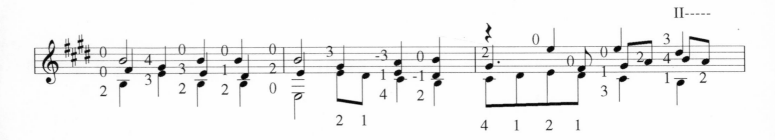

Early 5-course guitar housed in the Museu de la Música in Barcelona, Spain.

19. Ma bouche rit et mon coeur pleure

Jean Duboys

20. Il n'est plaisir ni passetemps

Clement Janequin

21. Notre dince, mon compere

Clement Janequin

25. Un jour un gallant engrossa

Pierre Certon

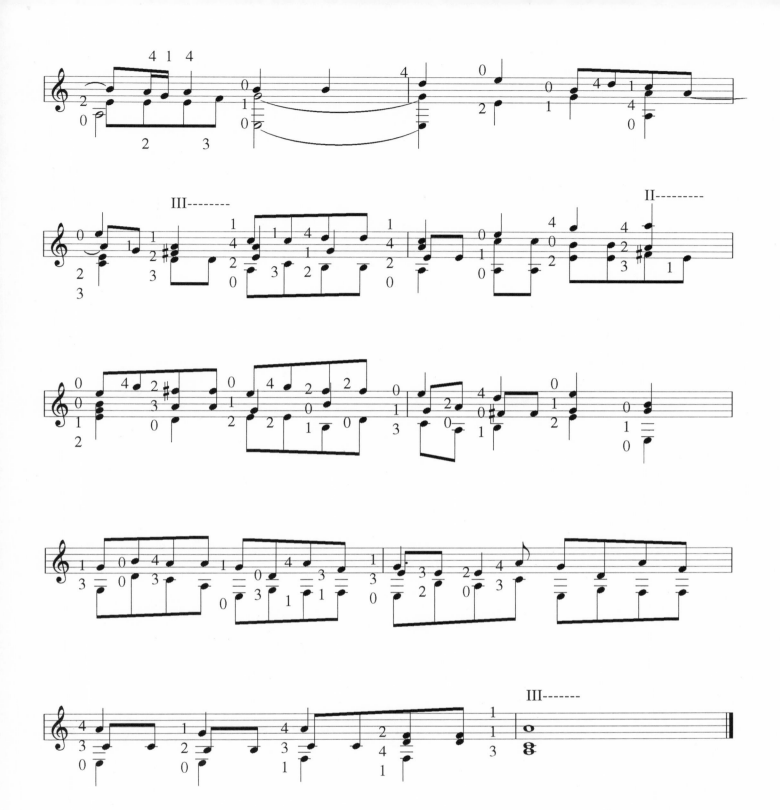

23. Pauvre coeur, tant il m'ennuie

24. Apporte a boire

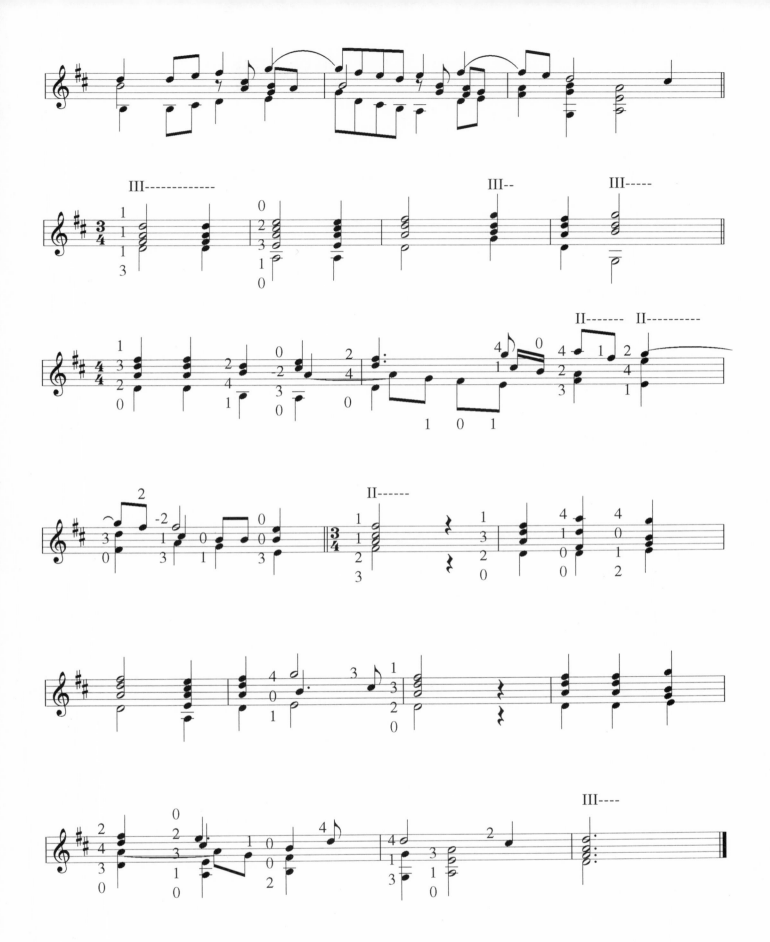

25. Reveillez vous, jeunes dames qui dormez

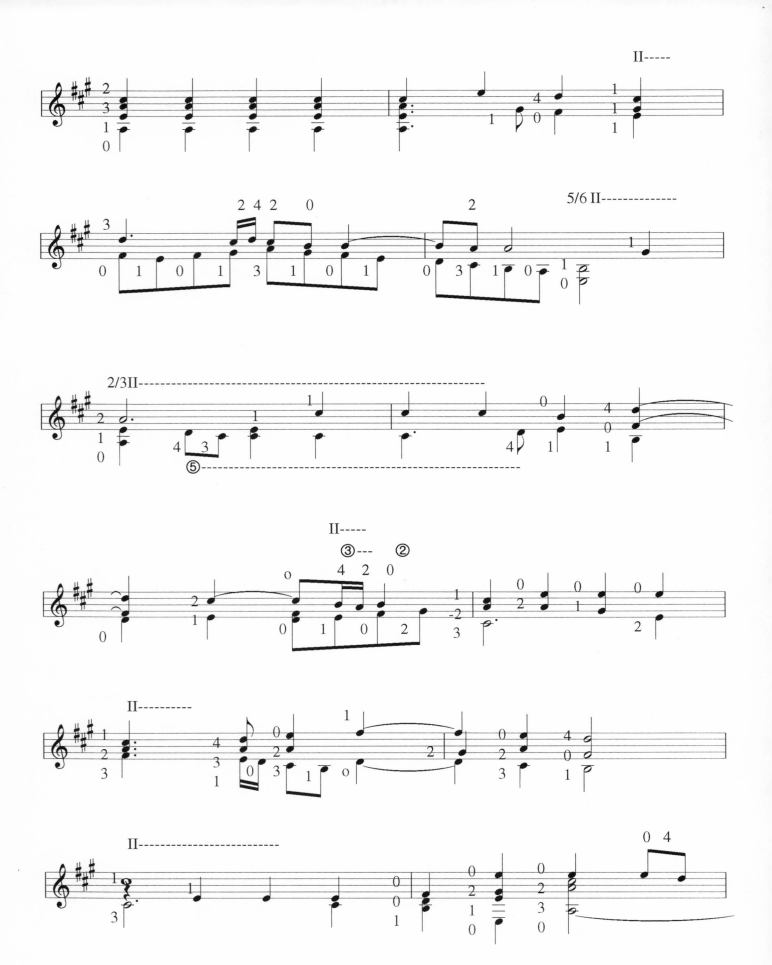

Additional Music from Other Sources

26. Ma bouche rit

Johannes Ockegham

(virelai)

27. Faulte d'argent

Josquin Desprez

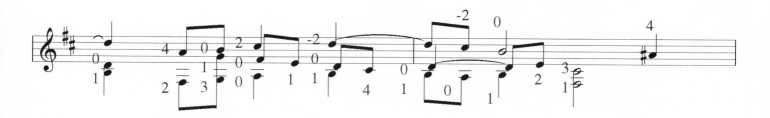

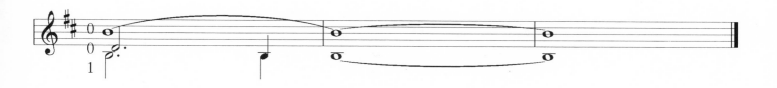

28. Tant que vivray

Claudin de Sermisy